A PORTFOLIO

OUTDOOR
FURNISHING
IDEAS

CONTENTS

Printed in U.S.A.
Library of Congress
Cataloging-in-Publication Data
Portfolio of outdoor furnishing ideas.
p. cm.

ISBN 0-86573-885-8 (softcover)
1. Outdoor furniture. 2. Interior decoration.
I. Cy DeCosse Incorporated.
NK2115.5.O87P67   1997
747'. 9—dc20

Author: Home How-To Institute™
Creative Director: William B. Jones
Associate Creative Director: Tim Himsel
Art Director: Ruth Eischens
Group Executive Editor: Paul Currie
Managing Editor: Carol Harvatin
Copy Editor: Janice Cauley
Contributing Editor: Andrew Sweet
Vice President of Photography & Production: Jim Bindas
Production Coordinator: Laura Hokkanen

Printed on American paper by Webcrafters Inc. (0996)

CY DeCOSSE INCORPORATED

COWLES
Creative Publishing

A Division of Cowles Enthusiast Media, Inc.

Chairman/CEO: Philip L. Penny
Chairman Emeritus: Cy DeCosse
President/COO: Nino Tarantino
Executive V.P./Editor-in-Chief: William B. Jones
99 98 97 96 / 5 4 3 2 1

Other Portfolio of Ideas books include:

A Portfolio of Kitchen Ideas

A Portfolio of Deck Ideas

A Portfolio of Landscape Ideas

A Portfolio of Bathroom Ideas

A Portfolio of Window & Window Treatment Ideas

A Portfolio of Flooring Ideas

A Portfolio of Bedroom Ideas

A Portfolio of Unique Deck Ideas

A Portfolio of Lighting Ideas

A Portfolio of Water Garden & Specialty Landscape Ideas

A Portfolio of Porch & Patio Ideas

A Portfolio of Storage Ideas

A Portfolio of Fireplace Ideas

A Portfolio of Ceramic & Natural Tile Ideas

A Portfolio of Fence & Gate Ideas

Photos on page two (top to bottom) courtesy of Winston
Furniture, Tropitone Furniture Co., and Dayva International.
Photos on page three (top to bottom) courtesy of Brown Jordan,
Country Casual, and Tropitone Furniture Co. Background photo
courtesy of Architectural Facades Unlimited, Inc.

WHAT ARE GREAT OUTDOOR FURNISHINGS?

Create an appealing atmosphere for a porch, patio or simply out on the lawn, and it's the place where everyone wants to be—to eat, play, lounge, chat and socialize. A great outdoor area originates from a space that is attractive and welcoming, and the furnishings are the tools you will use to pull it all together. Today you'll find an array of styles and designs to help you create an outdoor atmosphere that is a comfortably furnished and useful extension of your indoor living space. At the same time, outdoor furnishings enable you to express your personal style and create a setting that has a unified and tastefully finished look. Furnishing any outdoor space can enhance the value of your home, as well as the enjoyment you get from your outdoor environment.

Styles of outdoor furnishings range from vintage Victorian to simple Shaker, with many different options in between. The various styles of outdoor furniture designs allow you to create atmospheres from casual comfort to elaborate elegance. Materials range from aluminum and wrought iron to teak and redwood. A number of new materials, more durable and better suited for outdoor use, have dramatically expanded the selection of attractive outdoor furnishings now available. You'll find many fresh new styles and exciting new designs. With a little imagination you can transform an ordinary yard into an outdoor setting that is as comfortable for intimate get-togethers as it is for backyard barbecues. *A Portfolio of Outdoor Furnishing Ideas* features useful information and lots of idea-inspiring photos to help you create an inviting outdoor living area. With the right selections you can furnish an outdoor setting so that it combines the atmosphere, comfort and style you enjoy indoors, with the open-air appeal of the great outdoors.

A stylish, wrought-aluminum table set adds an international flair to this cozy outdoor courtyard. The setting features an intimate dining area and allows the homeowner to enjoy the outdoors in a comfortable and relaxed atmosphere.

Photo courtesy of Brown Jordan International

The sleek design of these sling chairs *enhances this relaxed, easygoing outdoor atmosphere. The high-back swivel rockers have a contoured frame with a canvas-covered padded sling that lets you enjoy outdoors in casual comfort.*

An attractive aluminum grouping features a large, shade-providing umbrella, made from the same colorful fabric used on the chairs. The strong structural design is perfect for the active and demanding use it will get in this outdoor patio area.

Planning

A thoughtfully furnished outdoor area, such as a patio, porch or deck, expands your usable living space by transforming it into a finished and functional outdoor room. You and your family will get more enjoyment from an outdoor space if you are as comfortable outside as you are inside. Choosing outdoor furnishings that coordinate with your interior space will visually link both areas together, creating a smooth transition between them.

Outdoor furnishings not only enhance the appearance of your home, they also allow you to express your own personal style. With the variety of options available, you can furnish and accessorize an outdoor area to create a stylish ambience anywhere. Romantic wrought-iron designs create a comfortable, cozy setting in a secluded garden. More contemporary lightweight designs, in aluminum or molded resin, sometimes called plastic, are perfect for furnishing a poolside patio or sunny deck that is busy with activity.

Handcrafted cast aluminum looks rustic, yet is rich in detail. This intricate grapevine design is reminiscent of the rugged beauty of the California wine country. This grouping adds a timeless elegance to this outdoor setting and blends perfectly with the exterior of the house and patio.

Outdoor furnishings can add a special ambience anywhere. An ordinary garden is transformed into a vintage Victorian-style setting with cast-aluminum furniture created to have the old-fashioned appeal of ornate cast iron.

The refined beauty of this teak garden bench creates the atmosphere of an elegant English garden. The handsome woodwork offers a comfortable and attractive place to sit, while providing a warm visual balance to the cool brick wall and stone-paved footpath.

Planning

CREATING AN OUTDOOR AMBIENCE

To create a comfortable, unified outdoor appeal, you must establish a certain mood, or ambience, in your setting. One of the most influential factors is the way you furnish your outdoor environment. The colors, materials, patterns, textures, furniture styles and frame finishes should also contribute to the ambience. You also need to consider how the various elements of your yard will blend together with the furnishings you select. Think about furnishing your outdoor space the same way you go about furnishing the interior of your home. With coordination and planning, you can produce an outdoor space that is as comfortable and gets as much use as any indoor space.

The types of activities you enjoy will influence the type of outdoor area you create. For example; areas that are host to water sports and other physical activities require durable, easy-to-move furniture, such as resin or aluminum. If peaceful moments or quiet conversations are more your style, choose furnishings with large sturdy frames and comfortable cushions, such as elegant wrought iron, handsome wood or wicker groupings.

Once you determine which furnishings best meet your activities, you need to decide what mood you want your outdoor area to project—romantic, sporty, festive, cozy, elegant? There are outdoor furnishing options available that can create almost any atmosphere imaginable. Bright white resin or painted wood furnishings offer a contemporary, yet casual, appearance. Ornate wrought iron or old-fashioned wicker creates an appealing old-fashioned elegance.

Featuring an interesting focal point as the centerpiece of the setting adds an element of interest, and influences the mood of the area. A focal point can be as simple as a birdbath, or as elaborate as a water garden with a fountain or a waterfall; even the furnishings themselves can become the central theme or focus of a setting. Accessories such as a sculpture or an elegant awning express an individual style, enhance your furnishings and become a part of the outdoor environment.

A cool, casual and contemporary effect is created by furnishing this poolside patio with innovative outdoor furniture designs. This five-piece dining set features high-backed swivel rockers on steel frames with sleek-looking sling seating. A large cloth umbrella coordinates the color scheme and provides soothing shade for this sunny poolside setting.

OUTDOOR FURNISHINGS FOR ANY ACTIVITY

Think carefully about the many ways your outdoor space will be used. The activities you enjoy will influence the types of furnishings you select, and the right furnishings can organize and define a functional outdoor setting. For example, someone who loves to sunbathe will furnish an outdoor space entirely differently than will someone who wants a comfortable spot to read a book or a formal setting for elaborate outdoor entertaining. A family with young children will have needs and priorities that differ from those of a household with no children.

Once you've determined the types of activities you enjoy in your outdoor space, choose outdoor furnishings that enhance these activities. If eating alfresco is one of your passions, furnishing your area to accommodate outdoor dining will most likely be a priority. Furniture choices that would work best in this setting include a dining table and chairs, an umbrella and perhaps a serving cart or love seat. Outdoor areas used for outdoor entertaining and socializing also need to be flexible enough to change with the style and scale of the gatherings. Large gatherings require lots of seating, as well as tables and serving accessories. On the other hand, if a quiet restful retreat is how you view your outdoor area, comfortable, cushy lounge chairs might be the outdoor furnishing of choice.

In addition to finding furnishings that fit the function, you must also choose a style that fits your personal taste. The visual impact of the furnishings will set the tone for the entire outdoor area. With the many options available, there is a style of outdoor furnishing that will enhance any atmosphere. Glass-topped tables are available in a variety of shapes and sizes. Chair designs ranging from old-fashioned wrought iron to modern European themes are available in a variety of materials, and support several seating choices to match your own sense of style. No matter what types of activities you use your outdoor furnishings for, you'll also need a convenient place to store certain items. Many types of outdoor furnishings are collapsible for easy storage.

Handcrafted wrought-iron furnishings create an elegant outdoor living room, complete with couch, coffee table, end table and ottoman. The attractive design of the furniture creates an attractive outdoor environment and expands the home's usable living space.

Photo courtesy of Meadowcraft

Photo courtesy of Brown Jordan International

(above) **Colorful teal-colored** cushions add a fashionable flair to this Mission-style teak furniture set. The simple styling is accommodating and comfortable for a number of activities, and the contemporary colors are an ideal match for the modern styling of this outdoor area.

(left) **Crisp white wicker** adds a Victorian flavor to this poolside setting. The specially made all-weather wicker is built to withstand natural wear. The flexibility of this functional dining group is enhanced by accessory items, such as a garden umbrella and tea cart, that make it possible for this setting to accommodate dining arrangements from intimate to elaborate.

11

The classic elegance and timeless beauty of wrought iron are re-created in durable welded steel. *Swivel rockers with thick cushions provide a comfortable place for friends and family to relax and enjoy the unique ambience of this picturesque patio.*

Photo courtesy of Homecrest Industries, Inc.

Planning

SOCIAL GATHERINGS

Social gatherings have a more festive flair when your outdoor setting is furnished with stylish outdoor furnishings. The incredible selection of designs and styles makes it easy to create a comfortable outdoor atmosphere for any type of social gathering.

Make sure you have the right types of furnishings for the kinds of activities you may want to include in your social gatherings. For example, poolside parties call for comfortable

waterproof cushions and lots of loungers for sunbathing. On the other hand, many social gatherings include dining outdoors. Whether it's a barbecue or a banquet, you'll require ample seating and tabletop space, as well as comfortable, easy-access chairs and places to set drinks. Coordinating accessories can be added to enhance the comfort of your outdoor area. Items like umbrellas and awnings bring soothing shade when a social gathering gets too much sun.

Coordinated outdoor furnishings *create visual unity among a number of separate activity areas around this sunny pool. The flowing curves and smooth lines of the sling styling blend beautifully with the contemporary style of this outdoor area. The sling seats are designed for comfort, while the fabric is cool and quick-drying.*

DINING OUTDOORS

Dining outdoors is much more enjoyable if the outdoor dining area is comfortable and well furnished. The furnishings you choose will depend on the type of dining you plan to do and the ambience you want the area to project. From boisterous backyard barbecues to quiet, formal candlelight dinners, the outdoor furnishings set the stage for whatever effect you're trying to create. You'll find outdoor furniture styles that are as formal or as informal as you desire.

In addition to dining sets, with the traditional table and chairs, there are a number of fun and functional outdoor accessories that will enhance dining and entertaining in any outdoor setting. Glass-topped tables are an outdoor favorite and are often the center of attention in an outdoor dining area. Classic and contemporary table designs are offered in circular, oval and rectangular shapes.

Attractive, easy-to-move serving carts enhance a desired design effect and simplify food service and preparation. Sufficient seating for outdoor dining is an important factor to consider. Sturdy chairs and benches make the most sense for outdoor dining. Other seating options, such as swings, love seats and hammocks, are ideal for a number of other activities, but aren't as effective for dining.

An interesting centerpiece for your outdoor setting can also add to the enjoyment of your outdoor dining area. Your options are wide open, as long as the piece you've chosen is visually pleasing and coordinates your outdoor design scheme. In a garden setting, a centerpiece of colorful flowers or attractive planting areas are effective options. In a more formal setting, such as a patio or a formal garden, an interesting sculpture or other artistic element is an excellent option.

Photo courtesy of Homecrest Industries, Inc.

The smooth, sleek look *of this outdoor dining set adds an air of sophistication to this poolside scene. Seating comfort is enhanced by padded cushions and the slight angle of the chair.*

Photo courtesy of Homecrest Industries, Inc.

Unique cushion detailing *makes this group a favorite for furnishing an outdoor dining area. The swivel rockers offer comfortable seating and make it easier to get to and from the table.*

An elegant, quality-crafted teak dining set creates a formal feel in this protected patio setting. The good looks, durability and weather-resistant qualities of teak furniture create an outdoor area that's as compelling and comfortable as any indoor dining area.

Wrought-iron furnishings *create a cozy, romantic setting, reminiscent of a sidewalk cafe. This sunny deck has been furnished with matching wrought-iron table sets. Using two smaller tables offers ample accommodations for drinking and dining. This arrangement also makes more efficient and flexible use of space than one larger table would.*

What could be more relaxing *than a luxurious lounge chair and a beautiful seaside setting? The slatted design of these loungers was created for function as well as beauty. The back is adjustable, and wooden wheels allow you to move your outdoor setting to another scenic location at any time.*

RELAXATION & SECLUSION

We all relax in different ways, such as reading, writing, sunbathing or even bird watching. Whatever method you use to unwind, outdoor furnishings enable you to relax in the natural surroundings and comfort of your own outdoor oasis.

There are many innovative furnishings specifically designed to promote comfort and relaxation outdoors. The variety of design and style choices in chaise lounges alone is amazing. They range from suspended hammocks that gently sway in the breeze under a favorite tree to contemporary resin designs that offer cool, comfortable poolside sunbathing. There are awnings and umbrellas that provide shelter from sunlight and a range of colorful pads and cushions for added seating comfort. Many accessories, like gliders, hammocks and swings, add the soothing sensation of motion to enhance ultimate relaxation. Whatever type of outdoor relaxation you enjoy, you'll find outdoor furnishings to fit your lifestyle.

Photo courtesy of Adirondack Designs

*The **Adirondack design** of this redwood chaise evokes the rustic feel of old-fashioned picnic tables and woodland campgrounds. The slatted construction of the chaise provides good air circulation. A standard-size cushion can be used for added comfort and color.*

*The **contoured shape** of these resin chaise longues accommodates sunbathers in cool comfort. The white resin looks crisp and clean without a cushion, or you can add a dash of color or a bit more comfort with an attractive cushion or pad.*

Photo courtesy of Triconfort

*A **multiposition** chaise longue is the ideal furnishing for ultimate relaxation on this picturesque poolside patio. The fluid lines of this attractive lacquered resin are enhanced with stylish and comfortable cushions. An attachable hood provides adjustable shade.*

Photo courtesy of Adirondack Designs

A secluded garden spot, surrounded by nature, might be where you choose to spend your quiet time. This Adirondack-style swing provides a comfortable and relaxing place to sit.

Swaying gently in a hammock is an excellent way to release the stress and tension from your body. This portable hammock stand enables you to enjoy the soothing sensation of rhythmic relaxation almost anywhere.

Planning

RELAXATION & SECLUSION

Relaxing outdoors can be as easy as finding a comfortable chair where you can sit and watch the world go by. All you really need in order to relax outdoors is a comfortable environment. If quiet and secluded is the atmosphere that pleases you, outdoor furnishings can help set the mood for your special sanctuary. In addition to the numerous chaise lounge options available, there are other outdoor furnishing options, such as benches, chairs, swings and love seats, that can enhance your outdoor relaxation. Sleek sling designs, smooth, polished wood and comfortable pads and cushions are some of the items especially for resting and relaxing outdoors.

There are a number of other fun and functional outdoor furnishings you can use to increase the comfort of an outdoor setting. For example, colorful umbrellas provide a shady spot in a sunny outdoor setting. Umbrellas and awnings can also provide privacy and a sense of seclusion in an otherwise busy backyard.

Rustic, natural-wood rockers create a setting that's a classic for many American porches. These comfortable rockers offer a pleasant place to sit and relax, any time of the day.

Outdoor relaxation rounds a corner *with this dignified, distinctive bench design. The graceful lines of this handsome bench issue a quiet invitation to sit and enjoy this beautiful outdoor setting with its lush scenery.*

CREATING FOCAL POINTS

An interesting focal point or centerpiece is a must for an outdoor setting. Any element that captures the center of attention and pulls the setting together can function as a focal point. Your choice can be as simple as a sundial or as elaborate as a flowing waterfall or fountain. A scenic view or even an attention-getting furniture setting can function as a focal point.

Look for a centerpiece that enhances the theme of your outdoor environment. If your outdoor setting doesn't have a natural focal point, you can easily create one. It doesn't have to be anything elaborate—a potted plant or small sculpture is enough to add an element of interest. There are a number of fun and functional outdoor accessories, such as decorative shelves, canopies or cleverly designed serving carts, that can also function as effective focal points in an outdoor area.

Outdoor lighting is an excellent way to create an unusual and interesting focal point in your outdoor area when your entertaining extends into the evening hours. Other ideas include planters, baskets, birdbaths, ponds, interesting trees, planting areas and flower gardens.

Photo courtesy of Summer Classics

This graceful garden setting *focuses on the beauty and tranquility of a formal water garden. Crafted from cast aluminum, this delicately detailed dining set offers an amazing amount of strength and durability, making it an ideal choice for elegant outdoor areas.*

(left) ***A weather-worn sundial*** *is the focal point for this formal garden. Handsomely designed welded aluminum furnishings complement the iodized iron sundial and enhance the elegant environment.*

(below) ***Coordinating wrought-iron accessories*** *function as attractive accents in this formal courtyard setting. The arched arbors and center planting bed are focal points that will capture more attention as they fill with colorful foliage.*

FINISHES & FABRICS

Finishes and fabrics for outdoor furnishings should be functional for the types of outdoor activities you enjoy. Improvements in materials make it easier to find the finish and fabric that are the best fit for these outdoor activities. New finishes are more durable and bond better to the frame, acting like a plastic skin that covers the frame. They are extremely weather-resistant and won't chip, crack, peel or fade. Improved outdoor fabrics are now made of a weather-resistant polyester/acrylic that has been treated with ultraviolet inhibitors, to reduce fading from the sun.

Metal furniture is a good choice for many outdoor activities, such as dining and entertaining. If a sophisticated outdoor setting is what you desire, an antique-looking finish on a metal frame adds a formal feel to an outdoor setting. Finishes range from antiqued, textured, mat or multicolored, to those that mimic stone or pewter. While many of these finishes protect the furniture from rust—beware of poor-quality metal frames that were given a coating of spray paint, instead of a rustproof finish.

Because resin is durable, easy to clean and relatively inexpensive, it makes a good choice for high-activity areas, especially those used by kids. Chemicals are added during the production of resin furniture to produce a finish that enhances the color and resists sun fading. The built-in finish also increases the strength of the resin and its resistance to dirt. Resin can be painted or lacquered to achieve a more sophisticated style.

Wood furniture adds a natural warmth to any area. Many wood designs have a sturdy, comfortable appeal that brings a feeling of strength and stability to an outdoor setting. Look for cedar or redwood, which is naturally resistant to decay, or wood that has been treated with a weather-resistant sealant. Wood can be finished with a clear sealant to maintain the original color, or it can be stained or painted. Another alternative is to let the wood age naturally, turning to a silvery gray. If you choose a paint finish for your wood, be aware that some maintenance is required.

In addition to providing additional protection from the elements, these frames and finishes are an important factor in creating a look that fits the function and style of an outdoor area.

The smooth, streamlined beauty of this welded aluminum furniture offers strength and sophistication. The design of the furnishings and the contemporary cushions create an elegant environment for this poolside patio.

(left) **Handcrafted cast aluminum** *creates an effect similar to the ornate cast-iron railing and garden furniture found throughout Europe. This furniture, however, is made of lightweight aluminum instead of heavy iron.*

(below) **Bright white resin furnishings** *add a crisp, fresh look to an outdoor area.*

(left) **Extruded resin is woven to look like wicker.** *This whimsical wicker dining set brings the flavor of the Far East into an outdoor environment. The weather-resistant resin stays comfortable and will not crack or peel.*

(below) **The appeal of natural wood** *has made it a favorite material for outdoor furnishings.*

(above) **This attractive aluminum table and chair set** *offers a traditional look in outdoor furnishings. The pastel print of the cushions pairs with the white finish of the aluminum to give this open-air setting a light, fresh feel.*

(inset right)
All-weather wicker *creates a comfortable, at-home atmosphere in any outdoor environment.*

FINDING THE RIGHT OUTDOOR FURNISHINGS

Some of the most popular materials for outdoor furnishings include aluminum, wicker, rattan, wrought iron and resin. There are aesthetic and structural differences, and advantages and disadvantages to each. Although wood requires more maintenance than other outdoor frame materials, it still has a popular appeal for use in outdoor areas. Unless treated, wood will weather to a soft silver color. This weathered look is soft and attractive, often the effect that is desired. Lightweight aluminum is one of the most popular materials for outdoor furnishings. Designs are now available in heavier grades of aluminum, and more pieces are being produced in wrought or cast aluminum to resemble wrought iron, which has a traditional, Old World look to it.

Woven wicker has expanded beyond its traditional look and feel. Wicker now spans a range of styles, weaves and colors to accommodate any outdoor ambience. Vinylized wicker produces weather-resistant furniture that holds up well under wear. Despite its reputation as a cheaper outdoor furnishing alternative, resin furniture is increasing in popularity because of its low cost and low-maintenance qualities. It is also increasing in popularity because resin designs are becoming more stylish and upscale. You can find resin furnishings with movable parts, comfortable shapes and appealing details.

For those who enjoy doing a bit of the work themselves, there are furniture kits available in some of the more traditional wood furniture styles, such as Shaker and Queen Anne. These kits include the pieces and the hardware, but require assembly and finishing. They offer the do-it-yourselfer an opportunity to furnish an outdoor area with quality outdoor pieces and save some money.

The style, design and structural composition of the seating are other distinctive qualities among outdoor furnishings. Sling, strap, cushion and bench are the most common seating options. Sling furniture, in which fabric is stretched or slung onto a frame, is a good choice for those who want outdoor furniture that is lightweight, low maintenance and stackable for easy storage. The quality of cushions for outdoor furnishings has also improved. New fabrics dry quicker, clean up easier and don't fade as fast as materials previously used.

A handsome metal bench brings to mind the casual elegance of a traditional English garden. Forged iron furnishings are as sturdy as they are charming.

Photo courtesy of Summer Classics

This traditional wrought-iron collection *has classic curves and elegant design. The deep teal finish featured here is an example of the extraordinary array of finishes that are now available for wrought-iron furnishings.*

Design

FRAME MATERIALS

Buying outdoor furnishings can be costly. To get the most for your money, it is important to stress quality in the choices you make, especially in the frames you choose. You can always change cushions, but the frames should last for years. The selection of frame materials in outdoor furniture runs the gamut from inexpensive vinyl to elegant, handcrafted teak and wrought iron. Differences in quality are not always apparent. Knowing how to evaluate the quality of different pieces allows you to choose the type of outdoor furnishings that will work best for your needs and those of your family.

When comparing frame materials, weight is an important sign of quality. A higher-quality piece will contain more material and be heavier than a piece in the same material that is of lesser quality. Better-quality furniture has more generous proportions. The seating space is roomier and the arms and legs are more substantial. Scrutinize the welds when looking over aluminum, metal and iron frames. The less apparent the welds, the better the quality. Manufacturers of the highest-quality, most-expensive lines will hand-grind all welds so they are invisible.

The color of the finish should be rich, deep and even. It should appear to be part of the frame material rather than a coating. If the finish is textured, it should be evenly textured everywhere, not more in one spot than another. If the finish is smooth, it should be flawless. The color coverage should be consistent and even. Cushions should have neat, well-defined corners or curves and tailored seams. The shape should be pleasantly plump, not squashed in appearance, which usually indicates insufficient stuffing. Furniture that features straps should have them double-wrapped around the frame. Double wrapping enhances resiliency and durability.

Take time to study the quality before you invest in expensive outdoor furnishings. There are many copies of quality furnishings that appear similar, but don't have the same detailing and geometry of design. The color choices are more limited and many fabrics and patterns offered by the top-quality manufacturers are not otherwise available.

*(left) **The light-and-airy look of wicker** is captured in weather-resistant resin. A special process uses extruded resin and wraps it around an aluminum frame to resemble real wicker.*

*(below) **Lacquered resin frames** produce a look that's clean and contemporary, with a distinctive finish.*

*(left) **Extruded aluminum frames** are combined with sling seat styling to produce outdoor furnishings with a classical Greek flair.*

*(below) **Teak garden furniture** creates a lovely outdoor living area on an open patch of lawn. A matching umbrella has a solid teak pole and comes in a variety of colors.*

ALUMINUM

Aluminum is a great outdoor material. It's relatively lightweight, so aluminum furnishings are easy to move, but still strong and durable. Aluminum doesn't rust and requires a minimum amount of maintenance. It will retain its good looks through the heat of the summer sun and drenching downpours. Good-quality aluminum furnishings can last for a decade or more.

There are three basic categories of aluminum—tubular, cast and wrought. Most aluminum furnishings are made from tubular aluminum, which is basically hollow tubing. The tubing is cut and bent to form the elements of the frame. The frame is then welded or bolted together. After the assembly is done, the frame is coated with a baked-on powder finish. Tubular aluminum is often found in contemporary aluminum furnishing designs.

Cast aluminum is produced by pouring molten aluminum into molds. Each casting mold is hand carved, which enables manufacturers to create the elaborate detail often seen in cast aluminum. The look of cast aluminum is distinctive and elegant. Many classic designs resemble the stylings of the 18th century. Cast aluminum can be costly, but if you want an elegant look that is durable and also easy to maintain, cast aluminum is ideal.

Wrought aluminum combines the look of handcrafted wrought iron with the lightweight, low-maintenance, high-tech qualities of modern aluminum. This material allows you to choose a style and a finish that have classic, elegant appeal, with the durability and comfort of modern-day technology. With wrought-aluminum furnishings, you can enjoy the traditional elegance of century-old wrought iron, in a material that is lightweight, low maintenance and rustproof.

Today, there are smooth, glossy or mat finishes, and finishes that resemble pewter or stone. Most are available in a wide range of colors. Some manufacturers offer aluminum furniture with a lacquer coating of kiln-baked polyester powder that adds extreme resistance in all conditions. These finishes enhance the durability of the frame because they are six times thicker than paint and highly resistant to weather. The finish becomes a plastic skin that bonds to the aluminum.

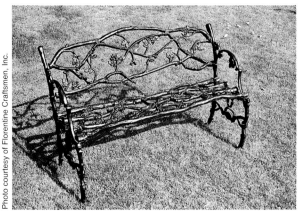

(above) **The delicate details** *of budding oak branches are captured in the design of this cast-aluminum bench.*

(right) **Low-maintenance aluminum mesh** *is a cool complement to these tubular aluminum frames. The corrosionproof aluminum is an attractive choice that's easy to maintain. Its good looks and durable, lightweight construction make aluminum an excellent value.*

(far left) **Cushioned comfort** *is combined with fashionable design and cost-conscious flexibility. This elegant dining set features "wrought-iron" styling in a contemporary aluminum creation.*

(left) **Cast aluminum takes on a distinctive design**. *The delightful shell-like shape of these chairs gives this outdoor area an elegant appeal.*

Light and lively aluminum *furnishings create a lovely outdoor setting. The lightweight aluminum can be easily moved or stacked for storage.*

WICKER & RATTAN

Wicker and rattan bring a natural handcrafted look to an outdoor setting. Today, the winsome look of wicker and rattan is available in styles that range from romantic to remarkably contemporary. Because natural wicker and rattan are susceptible to damage from exposure to the elements, sheltered settings such as porches and covered patios are the best locations for these materials.

Wicker itself is not a material, but actually a weaving technique. Natural wicker is handwoven from pliant strips of reed, but synthetic material can be used as well. Good-quality wicker feels smooth, with no splinters or loose ends that might catch clothing or start to unravel. The weave of the wicker should never be clogged with paint.

Natural wicker that is kept outside in a hot, dry climate should be sprayed with water once in a while. A new generation of "all-weather" wicker is taking the outdoor furniture market by storm. All-weather wicker is designed to be left outdoors. The frames for this type of wicker are usually aluminum, but the wicker itself is made of a number of durable materials, such as extruded resin, natural reed with heavy-duty coating, vinyl or fiberglass. Many of the all-weather wicker designs have a soft quality that often looks almost as natural as the original reed wicker and works well either indoors or out. You'll find sofas, day beds and lounges, as well as dining sets, service carts and storage pieces made of all-weather

(right) **A wonderfully wide selection** of *weatherproof wicker lets you enhance an outdoor living area with comfortable, stylish furnishings. Until recently, furnishings with this much style and comfort were reserved for indoor use only.*

Photo courtesy of Lexington Furniture Industries

wicker. These wicker materials can be hosed off every few weeks and cleaned occasionally with a mild detergent and water, if desired.

Rattan furniture creates a light, relaxed mood and can transform any setting, giving it an international flavor. Rattan, a palm stem, comes from the Far East. Like wicker, it is handwoven and is both durable and versatile in its natural state. The classic look of rattan works well in accent pieces, as well as in large groupings. Better-quality rattan has seat frames that are reinforced with hardwood corner blocks and extra bracing.

(left) **All-weather wicker** *is ideal for outdoor settings where moisture and direct sunlight are unavoidable.*

(below) **Traditional white wicker**—*what better way to enjoy the tropical breezes in this sheltered outdoor environment?*

(left) **Rich-looking, natural rattan** *adds a Far Eastern effect to this outdoor setting. An innovative shade-brella attaches to the railing and opens like a fan to create a sun, wind or privacy screen.*

(below) **Wicker takes a contemporary turn.** *Comfortable outdoor chairs combine the woven look of all-weather wicker with flexibility and motion.*

WOOD

The warm natural appeal of wood has always had a place in outdoor living areas like porches and patios. Wood furniture looks at home in almost any outdoor setting—on decks, patios, lawns, porches and in sun-rooms. Outdoor wood furniture comes in a variety of styles, with several durable finish options. Wood furnishings for outdoors are available in traditional as well as contemporary designs.

Many different types of wood are used to make outdoor furniture. Teak, cedar and redwood are the most common. Certain exotic hardwoods, such as cypress, jarrah and mahogany, are durable enough to be used for outdoor furnishings. The quality and cost of the furniture differs with the type of wood used, the design and the complexity of the joinery and the hardware used. The highest-quality products have a smooth surface and a tight grain, with mortise-and-tenon joints, wood dowels and brass or stainless steel hardware.

If you should choose wood for your outdoor furnishings, it will require some maintenance. And the durability and longevity will vary according to the wood type. One way to reduce the amount of maintenance your wood furniture requires is to allow it to weather naturally. If you choose not to oil or stain your outdoor wood furnishings, whatever the wood, they will weather to an attractive silver hue. If you want your wood furniture to keep its original color, you must reoil, restain or repaint every so often. Pieces like Adirondack chairs or front porch rockers are often painted. They require painting every year or so to stay looking sharp.

(right) **A delightful double rocker** *presents an inviting place to sit and gaze out as the ships go by. The mahogany wood was coated with a high-gloss, technologically advanced polyurethane finish that gives it incredible durability.*

(below) **Hand-carved designs** *can highlight wood furniture, like this floral pattern on a French Provincial style teak bench.*

Photo courtesy of Kingsley-Bate Ltd., Fairfax, VA

Photo courtesy of Weatherend Estate Furniture

*The **natural beauty of teak** is featured in the sleek, contemporary styling and smooth, wide lines of this design.*

*The **strength and warmth of rare African Bubinga** adds an exotic air to this setting. These pieces were coated with a varnish finish to enhance and protect the red color and pronounced grain.*

*This **handcrafted bent-willow chair** is an example of a beautiful traditional wood-furniture style found in the western North Carolina region.*

*An **octagonal market umbrella** uses solid teak as an attractive and effective material for the pole. The pole fits into a solid metal base that is easy to move and will fit neatly underneath a table.*

WOOD

The range of styles in outdoor wood furnishings runs from traditional country to Euro-style to contemporary. Some of the more classic outdoor designs include front porch rockers, classic garden benches and rustic Adirondack chairs and tables of every size and shape.

Outdoor furniture made of wood is very versatile; it can be dressed up or down with decorative cushions. Bright, vivid solids look carefree and colorful against the rich wood tones, while subtle prints can add a sense of sophistication.

(above) **Although this bentwood rocker** *has a rustic appeal, it also has a wonderfully sophisticated style. A colorful, Southwestern-style cushion adds a vibrant accent.*

The distinguished design of the wood table *turns this plain porch into an outdoor dining room. The matching benches and chairs can comfortably accommodate up to eight with ease.*

Enjoy the sights and sounds of the seaside *on this classic teak porch swing. This charming, painted swing features a slatted back and seat boards that let it be cool and help it dry quickly.*

Elegant teak furnishings *add the feel of the French countryside to almost any garden setting.*

The relaxing rhythm of an outdoor rocker *is enhanced by the comfort of the classic Adirondack design.*

A teak garden bench *adds an element of enchantment to any outdoor area. This beautiful bench features a backless design and delicate hand-carved detailing.*

IRON & STEEL

Some of the earliest styles of outdoor furnishings were fabricated with iron or steel. Iron and steel furnishings are versatile, stylish, strong and even sometimes less expensive than other outdoor furnishing frame materials. Furniture made from these materials is heavy and durable, yet is often adorned with graceful, flowing designs. It comes in a range of styles, from contemporary to traditional, which you can use to create comfortable outdoor settings on porches, lawns, decks and patios. The durability and heavy weight of steel furniture enable it to withstand high winds, driving snowstorms and years of abuse. It is almost indestructible.

Although iron and steel furnishings look similar, there are differences among the various materials. Tubular steel is made from pieces of hollow tubing that are bent and

Wrought iron creates a regal setting reminscent of the lavish life of the Roman empire.

Photo courtesy of Homecrest Industries, Inc.

(above) **This sturdy steel outdoor set** *features all-weather construction without compromising style.*

Advancements in material options allow you to enjoy furnishings like this fashionable steel dining set, with its elegant wrought-iron styling.

Garden-friendly green wrought-iron furnishings visually unify this formal garden setting.

shaped to create the frame. Designs made from this type of steel are often graceful and flowing. It may resemble furniture made from tubular aluminum, but it is always heavier.

Wrought-iron furniture is made from solid steel bars formed into designs, ranging from simple to ornate. It often has a classic styling that features appealing curves and elegant design elements. The versatility of wrought iron makes it as effective indoors as out.

Cast-iron furniture is heavy and ornate, and is often identified with the South. Because it is so heavy, cast iron is often used when you want to

This beautiful steel bench provides a peaceful retreat on this quiet patio. The fluted design is created by heating the steel, then running it through a die.

ensure that your outdoor furniture won't be moved. Iron pieces can often be three times as heavy as comparable aluminum chairs.

The selection of iron and steel pieces is almost endless. The variety of wrought-iron plant stands, baker's racks, shelving and specialty tables alone is enormous. And the range of colors and finishes is still growing. In addition to the traditional black, iron and steel furnishings are available in a wide variety of decorative new finishes, with white and forest green the most popular outdoor favorites. Many iron and steel seating groups can be used with or without cushions, opening the range of possibilities even more.

When making your iron and steel selections, look for a reputable manufacturer that promises a finish that inhibits rust and resists weather. Better-quality pieces made of iron or steel will be made with more parts than lower-priced versions. For example, the back legs of chairs and chaises of higher-quality iron and steel pieces will be reinforced with braces. Iron mesh will feel sturdy and be unrippled. Quality tabletops should slide into a channel that holds them in place, not be held in position by spot-welding around the edges.

When you get your furniture home, follow the care instructions carefully. Maintain steel furniture by washing it occasionally and applying liquid car wax at least once a year—two or three times is even better. If you see any rust, remove it with a wire brush and some touch-up paint.

RESIN

In the past, resin furniture, also known as plastic, has had a somewhat second-class reputation. It remained popular because it is relatively inexpensive and low-maintenance. Today, there is an entirely new generation of upscale resin furniture. These resin furnishings have been specially developed for the outdoors, so they are both practical and attractive. Today's resin furnishings have a more sophisticated style, but are still lightweight, low-maintenance, long-lasting and comparatively inexpensive.

Resin is actually polypropylene plastic that has had chemicals added to enhance its strength, resistance to dirt and fading caused by the sun. The furniture is produced by injecting plastic into a mold. Some furnishings are molded as one piece, making them very economical. Other pieces require the assembly of a few molded parts. Resin stays cool in the sun, handles water with ease and requires minimum maintenance. Because it is water-resistant, resin is ideally suited for use near water, as well as on lawns, decks, patios, porches or balconies. A simple wipe-down after a rain or a spill keeps it clean. A coat of paste wax, applied yearly, will help flat or satin-finish resin maintain its good looks. Because of its light weight, resin is not recommended for high-wind areas. A lacquer finish can be applied to resin, giving it a silkier, more sophisticated style.

The quality level among resin products varies and is often very apparent. Weight and size are two ways to judge the quality of resin products. A better-quality piece of resin furniture is usually heavier, roomier and more comfortable. Better-quality resin is also stronger, brighter and more resistant to the weather.

Resin furniture comes in a range of styles. There are designs that resemble traditional wood-slat styling, as well as a variety of contemporary designs and colors. While white is still the most popular color in resin furniture, it also comes a variety of colors. Resin furniture can be used without cushions, or you can add a splash of color with a comfy cushion or pad.

(right) **Waterproof resin** *is a wonderful material for this poolside setting. The contoured shape and slatted design of the furnishings help keep sunbathers cool and comfortable.*

Tubular resin gets it name from the tube-shaped PVC pipe. Originally, furniture made from PVC material looked much like the pipe it was made from. Today furniture made from PVC plastic comes in a variety of sophisticated styles and is as durable, low-maintenance and attractive as any type of plastic resin. It comes in a number of colors, and seating designs include cushion, strap or sling versions. It's also available in a full range of styles, from pieces that simulate the look of rattan or aluminum to those that emphasize the distinctive look of the material itself.

Photo courtesy of Allibert

Photo courtesy of Triconfort

An ideal outdoor material, resin is available in a variety of attractive and affordable colors and styles.

Remarkable new resin furnishings are ready for an afternoon social. This lively lacquered resin group adds a lovely, lighthearted style to the setting.

Photo courtesy of Allibert

Photo courtesy of Brown Jordan International

Resilient resin is woven over aluminum to create cool, comfortable all-weather wicker.

Photo courtesy of Triconfort

The contemporary character of this white lacquered resin maintains the light, elegant air of the scenic surroundings.

SEATING OPTIONS

There are many outdoor seating options that don't require a cushion or a pad. For example, wood, resin and furniture of certain metals, such as wrought iron, are often designed to be used with or without cushions. However, for comfort and a more contemporary look, there are three basic options available in seating styles for outdoor furnishings—cushion, sling or strap.

Before you invest in any type of outdoor seating, sit in the chair, lounge in the chaise or ride in the glider. You need to make sure the piece you choose meets your personal taste and comfort preferences. Also make sure it is functional for your outdoor lifestyle and the activities you enjoy.

The improved quality of acrylic and polyester fabrics for use with outdoor furnishings has produced fabrics that dry faster and are more resistant to fading. There are many lower-priced, look-alike products available, but the detailing won't be as intricate or elegant, the sizing will be less ample, the geometry of the design will be different and the choices in frame colors and fabrics will be limited. With an investment in quality now, you will be able to enjoy comfortable outdoor furnishings that will last for many seasons.

This rustic wrought-iron chair design relies on thick seat cushions for seating comfort. The fabric used to cover the cushions can be changed to give the setting a different look.

(left) **The cold, hard look of wrought iron** *is softened by the sophisticated style of the tailored cushions. These handcrafted wrought-iron pieces are ideal for all activity areas in this distinctive outdoor space.*

(below) **This artistically styled outdoor setting** *features an attractive array of sling seating. The straightforward frame designs include a variety of sling seating options, including conventional chairs, a swivel rocker, a two-seat glider and a four-position chaise.*

STRAP

Strap-style seating has a contemporary, clean look. Vinyl straps are wrapped tightly around and anchored to a sturdy frame that is usually made of aluminum or iron. Strap styles vary in design— they can be wide or narrow, wrapped horizontally, vertically or diagonally, or woven in a criss-cross pattern. Most manufacturers offer straps in a range of colors that coordinate with fabrics used on accompanying furnishings and accessories.

Straps are extremely durable, yet they are the least expensive seating option in outdoor furnishings. They require less care than cushions or slings and are easy to replace if you do happen to break one. The waterproof properties of vinyl make strap seating ideal for use around pool areas. Straps are also quite durable, making them a good choice in high-activity areas.

A good-quality strap will be fairly thick for durability, yet have enough give for comfort. It also comes back to its original form quickly after being stretched. Different manufacturers have different methods of attaching straps, such as nylon pins or double wrapping. Read the manufacturer's materials to determine which method you are most comfortable with. Remember, the way the straps are attached will affect the ease of future replacements.

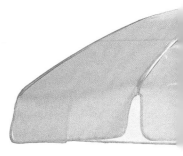

Photo courtesy of Brown Jordan International

(above) **This light-and-airy garden setting** *features the traditional furnishing style of wrought iron, combined with the contemporary comfort of vinyl straps.*

Photo courtesy of Winston Furniture

(above) **A whimsical, open-weave design** adds an unusual effect to this strap seating design. The deep green vinyl matches the green finish of the aluminum frame. From a distance, the vinyl straps give the illusion of being made of the same material as the frame, but a closer look reveals a much softer and more comfortable seating alternative.

(left) **This practical poolside setting** is furnished with classic strap seating. This traditional white strap design is one of the original, and still one of the most popular, outdoor furnishing options available.

Photo courtesy of Tropitone Furniture Co. Inc. and Dickinson Photography

SLING

Sling is the thing for lightweight, low-maintenance outdoor seating. Sling furniture is a seating style in which fabric is stretched, or slung, on a frame. The materials used for sling seating must be strong enough to resist sagging under the weight of an adult. Slings offer the best of both worlds, blending the simplicity of strap seating with the upscale look of fabric. Slings can be found in a variety of special blends of materials that look great, stay cool to the touch and are easier to care for than cushions. Most slings are made of open-meshed or specially woven fabric that is pulled taut across the seating area of a chair, bench or chaise, then attached to a special channel in the frame. The open-weave fabric allows water to pass right through for faster drying.

Slings are less expensive than cushions, but more expensive than straps. There is also a version that features a padded sling, which has a layer of polyester fill between two pieces of material. The frames for sling furnishings have a contemporary geometric look that is emphasized by the contour and curved shape of the sling.

A poolside patio *offers outdoor dining in casual comfort. This dining set features padded sling seats with a uniquely-shaped frame.*

Photo courtesy of Tropitone Furniture Co. Inc. and Dickinson Photography

Photo courtesy of Lloyd/Flanders Industries Inc.

(above) **This sophisticated sling seating** features neoclassical styling with a contemporary twist. The open weave of the sling fabric provides a comfortable, quick-drying seating surface.

(left) **Loosely woven, lightweight slings** offer cool, comfortable outdoor seating.

(below) **Simple, yet stylish.** Sling seating, with its down-to-earth design and lasting durability, is always a smart choice.

CUSHION

Cushions are the most expensive of the outdoor seating choices available, but they are also the most comfortable and one of the most versatile. Cushions add versatility; they can be changed any time you want to give your outdoor area a new look.

Cushions can be used to set the tone and establish a special ambience in an outdoor area. They come in different configurations, thicknesses, patterns and colors. Cushion styles range from clean, contemporary Euro-styles to tufted traditional looks.

Check the quality of construction— good-quality cushions should have well-defined corners or curves and neat, even stitching. The contour should be full and well shaped. Cushions can be filled with fiberfill, weather-resistant foam or alternating layers of both. A cushion that looks squashed usually has insufficient stuffing.

Cushions used outdoors are easy to care for and are easy to remove for cleaning and storage. They also drip-dry quickly if they are sprinkled by a hose or left in the rain.

Photo courtesy of Tropitone Furniture Co. Inc. and Dickinson Photography

White on white *is an ideal selection for this sunny outdoor setting. The streamlined design of the cushions complements the contemporary line and unique styling in the chair design.*

Photo courtesy of Tropitone Furniture Co. Inc. and Dickinson Photography

Carefully tailored cushions on this handsome teak furniture give this outdoor area an elegant interior quality.

Overstuffed cushions and the old-fashioned look of wicker create a cozy corner in this outdoor area.

These cushions, for the seat only, allow the elegant scroll design in this wrought-iron garden furniture to be admired from anywhere in the area. The black iron is accented by the colorful floral print cushions.

The distinctive design *of this charming portable tea cart matches the oversized sun chair and brings the ambience of an indoor den to this outdoor area. The handy cart features a recessed top shelf and an open lower shelf. Brass handles and rails add an elegant touch.*

Design

ACCESSORIES & ACCENTS

In an outdoor ambience, it is often the accessories that transform the area into an extension of your home. Whether you're furnishing a deck, patio, balcony or porch, it is the special touches, like planters, birdhouses, umbrellas, fountains and statues, that bring your personal touch to an outdoor area. Even the surrounding greenery becomes a part of your outdoor room. For example, a trellis covered with climbing clematis becomes a wall of color in an outdoor living room. Accessories bring an element of interest and excitement to an outdoor area. They are often highlighted and featured as focal points. Let your imagination run wild—with the right accents and accessories you can create an outdoor room that is as coordinated and comfortable as any space indoors.

The garden umbrella is one of America's favorite outdoor accessories. Health concerns regarding exposure to ultraviolet sunlight have increased interest in umbrellas and other sun-blocking accessories. Umbrellas, awnings and canopies can be distinctive elements of decoration. A unique umbrella, in an interesting style or vivid color, can give a unique spin to an outdoor space. Most umbrellas tilt, a convenient feature that permits you to control the amount of sun you receive. And umbrellas should always have a base of appropriate weight. An unanchored or unweighted umbrella can wreak havoc in a yard if it becomes airborne.

The colors and patterns available in outdoor accessories allow you to mix or match with the other elements of your outdoor decor. In addition to adding an element of style, awnings, canopies and umbrellas provide comforting shade from a hot summer sun. They come in almost any size, shape, fabric, construction and color imaginable. Some are made of open-weave materials that filter the sun and let air flow through. Others are designed with completely opaque fabrics and offer maximum protection from harmful sunlight.

Photo courtesy of Frontgate® Catalog

(left) **Protect your investment** *with outdoor furniture covers. High-quality waterproof covers will extend the life of your outdoor furnishings in even the toughest climates.*

(below) **An elegant outdoor canopy** *provides a shady retreat from the sun and heat. This stylish shade-producer is made of solid Rammin wood with beautiful brass-plated connectors.*

Photo courtesy of Dayva International

Photo courtesy of Lane Venture

(left) **Coordinated accessories** *make this cozy corner of the deck an attractive outdoor living room, complete with end table and ottoman.*
The open lattice and woven braid tailoring of this traditional wicker collection visually unify the outdoor area.

(below) **An impressive garden arbor** *gives you some control over the climate in your outdoor environment. The roof is waterproof and lined with an attractive awning. Draylon sliding curtains can be closed for additional shelter and privacy.*

Photo courtesy of Triconfort

ACCESSORIES & ACCENTS

Other outdoor accessories, like planters, benches, hammocks, trellises and arbors, add a special charm and serve as a focal point for an outdoor area. These types of outdoor accessories are not only attractive, but also can help you develop a look for your outdoor environment that is uniquely yours.

Dramatic lighting adds an artistic flair to an evening outdoors. Table lamps and hanging lanterns are just some of the many outdoor lighting options available. Candles also create instant atmosphere in almost any setting.

One of the most effective ways to use your outdoor space is to visually divide the yard into separate activity areas. By using outdoor furnishings and accessories, you can distinguish the different activity areas throughout your yard in a creative and artistic manner. A few carefully placed trees, flower beds and fences can frame different sections of an outdoor area. For example, a beautiful bench in a quiet corner of the garden creates a sheltered room, within the larger area, for resting and relaxing.

*A **combination of curved benches** makes a sweeping statement. The brilliant white bench adds a dramatic focal point that is intensified by this lush garden. The distinctive design of the bench makes it multifunctional—it adds an artistic landscape design element as well as a comfortable place to sit.*

An interesting variation of the distinctive Adirondack design style was used on this rustic love seat. A matching chair completes the traditional American setting.

An outdoor boot bench is the ideal storage accessory for a busy back porch. It also makes excellent storage for toys, sports gear and gardening tools.

Captivating curved benches capture the elegance of a seaside estate. A stunning slatted apron completes the distinctive design of this painted teak table.

An old-fashioned idea with contemporary comfort. A cushy sling-style swing sways gently within this stylish wooden frame. The freestanding design and attached awning provide a comfortable, portable shady spot to sit.

ACCESSORIES & ACCENTS

Decorative pots and planters are excellent outdoor accents. Garnished with colorful blooming plants, a unique pot or planter in a striking style can set the mood for an entire outdoor area. Ordinary items, like birdbaths and birdhouses, can become a part of a beautiful outdoor environment. They can be found in styles from Victorian to contemporary.

Many outdoor accessories are functional as well as fashionable. Colorful dishes, glasses, placemats and napkins can be coordinated with your outdoor decor to create a fun-filled setting for any season. Attractive accents and accessories can turn almost any outdoor entertaining event into a fun and festive affair. Lush greenery links any accessory to the natural beauty that surrounds it.

Simple yet elegant accessories, such as this appealing planter that matches the chair design, are the key to creating this picture-perfect porch. (inset) *Classic garden ornaments*, like these reproduction stone pots, bring a timeless elegance to an outdoor area.

An Italian wall fountain *adds international appeal to a special outdoor spot. This classic garden accessory is made of lightweight fiberglass with a limestone finish.*

Conifer topiaries *turn garden greenery into artistic elements. Various shapes and sizes allow you to style your living sculptures.*

An antiquelike terra-cotta finish *gives this lion urn and base an appealing, time-aged patina. The underlying material is actually lightweight fiberglass.*

The classic styling of this fluted urn *adds the grace and beauty of ancient Greece to any garden or outdoor area.*

Adding a decorative backyard birdhouse *allows you to enjoy the activity of nesting birds.*

An interesting shape *enhances the classic Victorian beauty of this plant stand.*

Teak wood planters *in a Provençal style are embellished with elegant round finials. These handsome carved planters are an ideal complement to any teak furnishings in the same outdoor space.*

The multifunctional modular design *of this bench and planter box combination allows you to create you own seating arrangement. The different configuration possibilities make this an attractive and versatile accessory for a deck or patio.*

ACCESSORIES & ACCENTS

Adding outdoor accessories can be as simple as adding another piece of furniture to an already established collection. An attractive shelf serves as storage, as well as a stylish outdoor accent. A gracious garden pond or fountain can function as the centerpiece for your outdoor setting.

(right) **Hand-tooled wrought iron** *adds an antique effect. This wonderful accent has water spouting from the beaks of three birds within this beautiful wall fountain.*

Photo courtesy of Florentine Craftsmen, Inc.

Photo courtesy of Brown Jordan International

A formal garden pond *adds a graceful accent to this outdoor setting. The beauty of the pond is enhanced by colorful ceramic tiles and an attractive urn and sculptures. The colors in the tiles and the cushion fabric can also be coordinated to visually unify the entire area.*

(left) **This attractive outdoor table and chair set** includes a matching baker's rack. This functional accessory can hold decorative accents or serve as effective storage.

(far left) **A beautiful stone birdbath** brings the quiet beauty and drama of a Japanese garden.

(left) **A cast-aluminum statue** creates the illusion of a beautiful woodland maiden who greets visitors to this garden.

55

A PORTFOLIO OF

OUTDOOR
FURNISHING
IDEAS

PORCHES

Porches are natural transition areas from the indoor home to the outdoor yard. Any porch can bridge these two distinct areas, but a great porch, with the right furnishings, will become a room unto itself, a special place to relax and enjoy a variety of activities.

If you have a large porch and wish to provide an elegant dining and entertaining experience, use wrought-metal furnishings to bring a strong, yet delicate, sense of style to your dining area.

For a softer, more natural appearance, wood is always a popular choice. A wooden porch swing or relaxing rocker is sure to become an instant favorite among family and friends.

And since porches are sheltered from the elements, you can use materials that otherwise might not be suitable for outdoor use. Wicker and rattan designs that are too delicate for full outdoor exposure will be right at home in a porch setting. Estate and garage sales are great places to find old tables and cabinets that can find new life as rustic porch accessories.

When planning decorating schemes, remember that a porch can be thought of as an outdoor room. Pillows, rugs, curtains and other hanging fabrics can be used to soften appearances and reinforce the cozy feel of a sheltered nook. Whether you are dining with guests or sharing coffee cake with a cherished friend, the right furnishings on your porch will help you comfortably enjoy this special area of the home.

Floral patterns *cut into the backs of these wrought-iron chairs echo the lush vegetation and trees nearby, and bring a delicate touch to this table set and matching planter.*

(right) **This stylish aluminum dining set,** *supported by brick pavers underfoot, allows the owners of this large, Spanish-influenced porch to enjoy graceful outdoor dining whenever they wish.*

(bottom) **Delicate but strong,** *this wrought-iron chair and table set is perfect for light snacks or an impromptu tea. The table and chairs fold for convenient storage and are precoated with polyurethane for protection against rusting.*

Weatherized wicker, resistant to moisture and sun, is the foundation for a comfortable yet formal dining experience on this sunny, spacious porch.

Photo courtesy of Lexington Furniture Industries

(right) **The muted patina** of this cast-aluminum table and chair set blends in perfectly with the creeping ivy and nearby trees. Generous cushions ensure long-lasting comfort, and the heavy glass tabletop is safe beneath the brick ceiling overhead.

(above) **Natural teak tables** combine with a bench and chair to create an inviting space on this large, open porch, and assorted flowers add a dash of color.

(left) **A year-round sun porch** becomes as cozy as any living room with the help of this wooden set. The teak color matches the wooden ledge surrounding the porch and boldly contrasts with the darker brick underfoot.

Classic wooden director's chairs, *here updated with bright colors, are a great informal seating option for the porch. They're light and portable, so you can make last-minute arrangements with ease.*

(above) **Enjoy the lazy days of summer** *on the porch in old-fashioned wooden rocking chairs, shown here in single and double-seat styles with a painted finish. Perfect for relaxing, socializing or just daydreaming, these chairs are sure to become family favorites.*

(left) **These delicate mesh-backed chairs,** made of wrought iron, are both comfortable and beautiful. The assorted planters and matching furnishings blend in harmoniously with the classic appeal of this southern porch. The wire shelves help make the porch seem more like an indoor space, and the handy wheeled cart accommodates garden tools as easily as it does refreshments.

(below) **These teak rocking chairs** are right at home under this sheltered wooden porch, which overlooks a nearby lake. The inviting rockers provide a great reason to stop and enjoy the fresh air and panoramic view.

Photo courtesy of Telescope Casual Furniture

PATIOS

A properly furnished patio can be the hallmark of an outdoor living area. Patios are used for a variety of activities, from simple relaxing to hosting an outdoor fiesta. The type of furnishings you choose for your patio should be versatile enough to accommodate different occasions, yet expressive enough to help you create a style you'll enjoy.

Patio furniture is constantly exposed to the elements, so it must be durable. To prolong the life of your furniture, store tables and chairs indoors during winter. Or use protective vinyl coverings for extra shelter. If outdoor cooking is planned, keep in mind that the furniture should be suitable for dining, comfortable and easy to clean. And you can always update your choice of cushion fabric as styles and needs change.

If you need numerous chairs for entertaining, you might opt for a less expensive ensemble in order to preserve a unified look. Or, if you like, express yourself by mixing and matching styles, allowing you to add different items as needed.

Cast-iron and aluminum furnishings have a classic, antique appeal that brings a formal tone to an outdoor area. For a more casual setting, cushioned recliners made of tubular aluminum are stylish and comfortable. Resin furnishings are practical and economical, and stacking plastic chairs also store conveniently during winter months. And the casual elegance of a wood dining set is a welcome addition to any patio. Whatever your needs, there's a style to help you get the most out of your patio.

Soft floral print cushions *and interwoven backstraps on the chairs in this dining set ensure that friends will enjoy this cozy, sun-drenched patio in style.*

69

Photo courtesy of Summer Classics

(left) **This delicate wrought-iron pattern,** replicated from a 19th-century French design, is perfectly at home on this flagstone patio. The faux stone table and fine white detailing contrast elegantly with the dense forest surroundings.

Photo courtesy of Wood Classics, Inc.

(above) **A innovative update** on a classic American design, these Adirondack chairs feature gently curved seats for maximum comfort and provide a great way to enjoy autumn's exploding colors. Generous armrests are wide enough to support refreshments, sunglasses or a favorite book.

(left) **Guests on this outdoor deck** can enjoy a view of a backyard pond from these amply padded aluminum chairs, which come in stationary and swivel models. A large, adjustable umbrella offers welcome shade on hot, sunny days.

(above) **These sleek folding chairs** *are sure to be a hit at your next outdoor meal. Constructed of lightweight aluminum, they are easy to store and look great under the wood-framed market umbrella.*

(right) **Pure white fabric***, modern steel framework and a frosted glass tabletop all combine in this functional dining set to create a bold design statement on this lakeside overlook.*

(right) **Weather-resistant wicker,** wrapped around aluminum frames, provides comfortable seating for this foreground dining set. Wicker easy chairs closer to the porch offer a relaxing spot for after meals, and both styles could be color-coordinated to match your sense of style.

Photo courtesy of Winston Furniture

Photo courtesy of Lloyd/Flanders Industries Inc.

Photo courtesy of Winston Furniture

(above) **Aluminum, not wood,** *is used in this lightweight Mission-style chair set. The matching cushions and umbrella fabric add to the classic Eastern Seaboard feeling of this lake setting.*

(below) **Cake and fruit cocktails** *become extra special for kids when enjoyed outdoors. The spacious glass tabletop will withstand constant use and cleans easily. The nearby wrought-iron fence ensures safety for everyone, while preserving a clear view of the water.*

(above) **This lush dining area** *takes special advantage of the setting sun and is a favorite spot for entertaining guests. A whitewashed terra-cotta planter suggests a classical flavor, while the textured cushions and frosted glass tabletop beautifully complement the house's stucco trim.*

(right) **Chairs, planters,** *dining tables and end tables furnish the front entrance of this large estate. These durable wrought-iron pieces are sturdy and heavy, yet visually appear light and airy, which helps them effectively offset the imposing heaviness of the nearby columns and railings.*

POOLSIDE

Poolside furniture provides a necessary and convenient place to rest and dry off from the fun and activity of swimming and playing in the water. Good pool furniture should also be versatile, providing comfort for those relaxing as well as practicality for those swimming.

Aluminum and resin are popular choices that won't rot or rust, although wood chairs and lounges can also be used with care. Cushions may be desirable, especially on metal chairs which could get hot in direct sunlight.

Several styles of strap and sling materials are available. These dry easily without sacrificing comfort. Avoid sharp edges on pool furniture, and consider adjustable models that can take full advantage of the changing position of the sun.

If you are dining by the pool, get ready for a stylish experience. The shimmering reflection of a pool provides the perfect accompaniment to receptions, dinners and parties, and beautiful furnishings will heighten the overall ambience even more.

Poolside furniture for entertaining should be portable, so different entertainment arrangements can be easily accommodated, and so items may be cleared away for swimming. Dining carts are a great help for bringing food to guests, since the outdoor grill may be some distance away. And large "market" umbrellas give adequate shade for a large table, ensuring that everyone has a pleasurable day by the pool.

These sling-backed chairs and the shady umbrella, coordinated to match the poolside paving tile, make a welcome resting spot for swimmers and can easily support a full outdoor lunch or dinner.

(right) **Slim and sensible,** the cushions on these durable steel chairs offer more support than basic sling seats, yet dry faster than more heavily padded cushions.

(above) **This wheeled lounge** with matching table creates a comfortable and portable place to soak up the sun or enjoy the morning paper. Stylish cushions provide added comfort for relaxing, and the folding umbrella expands to give shade when desired.

(left) **When comfort is a priority,** these steel rocking loungers with large, sumptuous cushions will ensure that everyone has an enjoyable time by the pool. The large, shady umbrella is coordinated to match the color of the surrounding tile, and the nearby loungers easily accommodate an afternoon nap.

(above) **This secluded corner** *of a long pool takes advantage of dining away from the center of pool activity. The resin furnishings are durable and weather-resistant, and the lightweight construction means you can rearrange the furnishings quickly and easily.*

Constant exposure to moisture *is not a problem for this coated aluminum table set. The baked-on coating, shown here in a lush green, comes in a variety of colors for every setting. The vinyl chair straps dry quickly and let water drip away, while an adjustable umbrella keeps everyone in the shade.*

This ultrasleek pool area features aluminum furniture with quick-drying strap seating, color-coordinated to perfectly match the blue and white border surrounding the pool and hot tub.

Photo courtesy of Tropitone Furniture Co. Inc. and Dickinson Photography

(above) **After a dip in the hot tub,** *relax under this spacious umbrella in a sling-cushioned chair or lounger, and take in the activity of the nearby marina.*

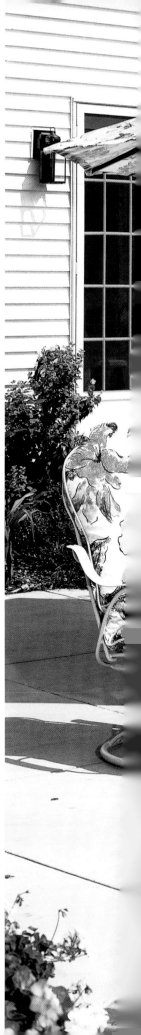

(above) **A cozy, informal spot** *for drinks or snacks benefits from the comfort and portability of resin furnishings. The umbrella adds a floral dash of color, and the drink cart makes entertaining simple and easy.*

(right) **Delicate wrought-iron framing** *is teamed with generous cushioning to create a comfortable dining spot under a broad market umbrella. A small fountain in the pool area lets guests enjoy the soothing sound of bubbling water.*

LAWNS & GARDENS

Creating a wonderful garden space is a rewarding experience, and with the right furnishings on hand, you can share your efforts with friends in comfort and style. Teak and cedar wood are favorite materials for lawn and garden furnishings. Wooden benches and chairs blend in with nearby foliage and bring a casual, yet distinctive, atmosphere to a particular area. They can be sealed, stained, painted or left to weather naturally, depending on your tastes.

If you desire a more formal sitting area, an ornate cast-metal table and chairs create an elegant spot for afternoon tea or socializing. The intricate metalwork always creates an interesting contrast to lush surroundings. Take care to ensure that narrow metal legs won't sink into soft ground.

Other accessories like birdbaths, pedestals, statues and sundials evoke the atmosphere of regal gardens of the past. Box or clay planters are another great way to focus attention on a specific area, or on a favorite type of flower. They can also provide that needed visual complement to a lone bench or chair.

Think of outdoor furniture as a landscaping tool. You can easily combine an inspiring lake view or a unique rock formation with a chair grouping. Or try using a favorite bench as a destination at the end of a serene footpath. Whatever your choice, enhancing your lawn or garden with the right furnishings will help you create a relaxing, comfortable retreat right in your own backyard.

Anchored by a turret-style *storage shed, the secluded corner of this yard plays host to a bright, casually styled furniture set. The nearby flowers and comfortable chairs create a great place to enjoy some refreshments and marvel at your garden's progress.*

PORTFOLIO

Photo courtesy of Classic Garden Ornaments, Inc. & Pennoyer Castings

(right) **This unique resin cast birdbath,** *lighter than stone or concrete and just as weather-resistant, is a delightful focal point and conversation piece for your garden or lawn. The birds will appreciate it, too.*

Photo courtesy of Moultrie Manufacturing Company

A circular cast-aluminum bench provides a shady resting place, highlights the tree and acts as a visual balance to the table and chair set nearby. The intricate patterns of these furnishings are right at home on this carefully manicured lawn.

(above) **Trellises and arbors** *establish an ornate architectural framework for this beautiful garden, attracting the eye and setting off the lush greenery. This intricate arched arbor houses a French-designed chair and table set made of woven and welded steel. The arch supplies a structural context for the furnishings, creating an extra-special place for dining or socializing.*

Painted white oak chairs *and plaid cushions with matching umbrella add to the country atmosphere of this garden nook. Placing plants on small tables like the one in the corner helps integrate the dining pieces with the flowering greenery nearby.*

(above) **A meandering footpath** *leads to this cozy dining area nestled in a variety of flowers and ferns. The barrel-back wrought-iron chairs are large and spacious, and cushioned for extra comfort. The plants and nearby trees act as natural sunshades for this spot, filtering and softening the incoming sunlight.*

(right) **The lattice design** of this intriguing teak ensemble was inspired by 18th-century Chinese motifs. The placement of this set takes full advantage of the nearby plant-covered wall, which provides a beautiful organic backdrop for enjoying tea, a light snack or a good book.

Photo courtesy of Geebro Ltd.

Photo courtesy of Weatherend Estate Furniture

(above) **An enchanting and secluded** garden retreat is accented by this single circular chair, which encompasses one of the arbor supports. Visually striking as well as comfortable, this chair is one that everyone will remember and enjoy.

This contemporary dining set blends harmoniously with the green lawn and bold architectural design of the house and is flexible enough for casual everyday use, as well as more formal occasions. The wide umbrella offers shade and also provides a necessary focal anchor for the set, highlighting this area against the large house behind it.

LIST OF CONTRIBUTORS

We'd like to thank the following companies for providing the photographs used in this book:

Adirondack Designs
350 Cypress Street
Fort Bragg, CA 95437
(707) 964-4940

Allibert
12200 Herbert Wayne Court, Suite 180
Huntersville, NC 28078
(800) 258-5619

Architectural Facades
Unlimited, Inc.
1990 Stone Avenue
San Jose, CA 95125
(408) 298-2758

Brown Jordan International
9860 Gidley Street
El Monte, CA 91731
(818) 443-8971 ext. 217

Classic Garden Ornaments, Inc.
Manufacturers of Pennoyer Castings
274 Glen Head Road
Glen Head, NY 11545
(516) 676-6236

Classic Garden Ornaments, Ltd.
makers of Longshadow® planters
83 Longshadow Lane
Pomona, IL 62975
(618) 893-4831

Country Casual
17317 Germantown Road
Germantown, MD 20874
Send $3 for a 72-pg. full color
catalogue of teak garden furniture.

Currey & Company
200 Ottley Drive
Atlanta, GA 30324
(404) 885-1444

Dayva International
7642 Windfield Drive
Huntington Beach, CA 92009
(714) 842-9697

Florentine Craftsmen, Inc.
46-24 28th Street
Long Island City, NY 11101
(718) 937-7632

Frontgate
Cinmar, L.P.
2800 Henkle Drive
Lebanon, OH 45036
(800) 626-6488

Gardenside, Ltd.
999 Andersen Drive, Suite 140
San Rafael, CA 94901
phone: (415) 455-4500
fax: (415) 455-4505

Geebro Ltd.
2145 Barret Park Drive, Suite 107
Kennesaw, GA 30144
(404) 419-7343

Hatteras Hammocks, Inc.®
P.O. Box 1602
Greenville, NC 27835
(800) 334-1078

Homecrest Industries®, Inc.
P.O. Box 350
Wadena, MN 56482
(218) 631-1000

Kingsley-Bate, Ltd.
5587-B Guinea Road
Fairfax, VA 22032
(703) 978-7200

La Lune Collection
930 East Burleigh Street
Milwaukee, WI 53212
phone: (414) 263-5300
fax: (414) 263-5508

Lane Venture
P.O. Box 849
Conover, NC 28613
(800) 447-4700

Lexington Furniture Industries
P.O. Box 1008
Lexington, NC 27293-1008
(704) 249-5300

Lloyd/Flanders Industries Inc.
P.O. Box 550
Menominee, MI 49858
(906) 863-4491

Meadowcraft
1401 Meadowcraft Road
Birmingham, AL 35215
(205) 853-2220

Moultrie Manufacturing Company
P.O. Box 1179
Moultrie, GA 31768
(800) 841-8674

O.W. Lee Co., Inc.
930 N. Todd Avenue
P.O. Box 880
Azusa, CA 91702
(800) 776-9533

Southerlands, Inc.
9 Pack Square SW, Suite 100
Asheville, NC 28801
(704) 252-5130

Stone Forest Inc.
P.O. Box 2840
Santa Fe, NM 87504
(505) 986-8883

Summer Classics
P.O. Box 1090
Pelham, AL 35124
(205) 663-1688

Telescope Casual Furniture
85 Church Street
Granville, NY 12832
(518) 642-1100 ext. 264

Triconfort
12200 Herbert Wayne Court, Suite 180
Huntersville, NC 28078
(800) 833-9390

Tropitone Furniture Co. Inc.
1401 Commerce Blvd.
Sarasota, FL 34243
(941) 355-2715

Weatherend Estate Furniture
6 Gordon Drive
Rockland, ME 04841
(207) 596-6483

Winston Furniture Company, Inc.
P.O. Box 868
Haleyville, AL 35565
(205) 486-9211

Wood Classics, Inc.
Box 6VB
Gardiner, NY 12525
(914) 255-5599